When Mission Meets Money

FINANCIAL GUIDANCE FOR MEDICAL NONPROFIT LEADERS

Matt Paprocki, JD, CFA, CFP®

AAPL

978-1-960762-49-8 Print
978-1-960762-50-4 eBook
Published by **American Association for Physician Leadership, Inc.**
PO Box 96503 | BMB 97493 | Washington, DC 20090-6503

Website: www.physicianleaders.org

13 8 7 6 5 4 3 2 1
Copyedited, typeset, indexed, and printed in the United States of America

PUBLISHER
Nancy Collins

PRODUCTION MANAGER
Jennifer Weiss

DESIGN & LAYOUT
Carter Publishing Studio

COPYEDITOR
Patricia George

TABLE OF CONTENTS

ABOUT THE AUTHOR

Matt Paprocki is a registered Investment Advisor Representative, Certified Financial Planner®, holder of the right to use the Chartered Financial Analyst® designation, and a member of the CFA Society of Chicago.[1] Paprocki graduated from Wheaton College with a bachelor's degree in business/economics and is a licensed attorney in Illinois. He earned his Juris Doctor from DePaul University College of Law, where he graduated magna cum laude, was elected to the Order of the Coif, and served on the DePaul Law Review as assistant executive editor.

Paprocki focuses on providing analysis and guidance regarding investment management strategies for nonprofit organizations as part of MEDIQUS's Institutional division. As of the start of 2026, he works closely with and advises nearly 100 nonprofit organizations. He has written white papers and articles about topics such as the benefits of establishing a reserve fund, the importance of a sound investment policy statement, and efficient methods for charitable gifting.

DISCLOSURES

This book contains general information that is not suitable nor applicable for everyone and was prepared solely for informational purposes. Nothing contained herein should be construed as personal investment advice nor does MEDIQUS Asset Advisors, Inc., or Matt Paprocki endorse the purchase or sale of any security mentioned. MEDIQUS Asset Advisors, Inc., is a registered investment adviser of which Matt Paprocki is an investor. For additional information about MEDIQUS Asset Advisors, Inc., including its services and fees, please request the firm's disclosure brochure using the contact information contained herein or visit advisorinfo.sec.gov. Investing involves the risk of loss of principal.

Past performance isn't indicative of future performance. Neither Matt Paprocki nor MEDIQUS Asset Advisors, Inc., provide legal or tax advice. You should contact your attorney or accountant for said advice.

This includes several case studies which are included for illustrative purposes only, to provide examples of the MEDIQUS Asset Advisors, Inc.'s process and methodology. The results portrayed in these case studies are not representative of all of the firm's clients or the clients' experiences.

This also contains certain forward-looking statements that indicate future possibilities. Due to known and unknown risks, other uncertainties and factors, actual results may differ materially.

ACKNOWLEDGMENTS

I would like to thank my wife, Rebecca, and my daughter, Hallie, for their endless love, patience, and encouragement. Their support has been the foundation that made this work possible. I am also deeply grateful to my family for their constant belief in me and for the many ways they have shaped who I am.

To the MEDIQUS team, thank you for your support, collaboration, and for helping me grow both personally and professionally. Your insight and encouragement have been invaluable throughout this journey.

INTRODUCTION

"A few people of integrity can go a long way."
– Bill Kauth, Co-Founder of The Mankind Project

Dr. Elizabeth Chen[2] pulls up the email reminder about today's American Society of Hospitalists (ASH) board meeting. She winces when she reads that the Investment Committee Report is the only topic on the agenda. (Investing is *not* an area in which Dr. Chen feels competent.)

She's nervous. Not only is it her first board meeting, but she's also a minute late!

She clicks the Zoom link and nods at the nine faces on her screen. She recognizes Dr. Raymond Johnson, a respected hospitalist from rural Georgia. She also knows Dr. Rebecca Goldstein, who heads a major hospitalist program in Chicago.

Board Chair Dr. Alex Rivera smiles broadly. "Dr. Chen! Welcome!" After a brief, informal introduction, he says, "Okay, just one item today. We're looking at our investment performance. Craig, the floor is all yours."

Dr. Craig Veerman, the board treasurer, shares his screen: a series of declining graphs.

"As you can see, our investments have lagged behind their benchmarks for the third straight quarter," he says somberly. "This begs the question, 'Is our strategy still serving our mission?' With rising operational costs and expanding program needs, the consensus of the investment committee is that we may need to rethink our long-standing approach."

"Well, it's about time!" Dr. Stephen Plette blurts out. (He's the academic director of the hospitalist program at a top medical school on the West Coast.) "Other organizations I've seen have much better returns. Personally, I think *everything* should be on the table — even crypto. Obviously, when we get better returns, we can do bigger things."

The group's executive director, Sarah Martinez, steps into the tension. She's been with ASH for only a few months, but she's already impressed everyone with her financial acumen and deft people skills.

"Dr. Plette is right in pointing out that our investments affect our ability to fund grants, education programs, and key initiatives," she begins.

"Which is why," Dr. Rivera interrupts, "we've got to approach these *financial* decisions with the same care we apply to all our *medical* decisions. Look, I don't know about crypto, but Dr. Plette's proposal deserves consideration. Of course, we also need to remember that the more we make, the more we can do with the organization's funds."

Others weigh in. As Dr. Chen listens to her fellow board members debate the pros and cons of various investment approaches, she feels somewhat lost. Yet the weight of the group's responsibility is not lost on her.

This is SO much bigger than one nonprofit's financial health, she thinks. *What we decide here will affect the advancement of hospital medicine for years to come.*

THE CHALLENGES IN STEWARDING A NONPROFIT'S FINANCES

The board members of every nonprofit face a host of challenges. On top of their already busy lives, they've agreed to manage, safeguard, and grow an organization's financial resources so that it can carry out its critical initiatives.

No wonder so many are like Dr. Chen. They say (or think) things like, "My expertise is medicine, not finance. And that's true of my fellow board members, too. We're all intelligent people, but let's face it ... We don't know the things we don't know. So, how can we be sure we're doing the right things ... making the best financial decisions?"

We believe board members must reckon with four realities if they are to provide healthy financial stewardship for their nonprofits.

1. The Weight of Fiduciary Responsibility

Being a board member means carrying a great burden. *You and your colleagues are the legal guardians of your organization's financial resources.*

That means "board member" is far more than a title or ceremonial role. It comes with serious legal and ethical obligations. Investment decisions (or indecision) affect an organization's ability to fulfill its mission. In some instances, board members have been held personally liable for reckless financial decisions that failed to meet the standard of prudent oversight.[3]

The stakes for medical nonprofits are high. Each one's ability to provide healthcare services, support medical research, and advance crucial healthcare initiatives is tied directly to its financial health and stability.

A single financial decision can impact a group's mission-driven work positively or negatively for years. A misguided move can curtail donations and services. A wise investment can change lives in amazing ways.

In short, being a fiduciary carries greater weight.

A second challenge is...

2. The Reality of Time Constraints

Most medical nonprofit board members are accomplished professionals in the medical field. They have demanding careers. They work long hours treating patients, doing important research, or teaching at medical schools. Some run smaller practices. Others manage larger healthcare entities. Their days are filled with administrative responsibilities and, in some cases, life-or-death medical decisions.

Agreeing to provide leadership and financial oversight to a medical nonprofit creates an additional set of pressures. To be effective, board members must give careful attention to organizational and financial details, participate in constructive dialogue, engage in insightful analysis of problems and opportunities, and use wisdom in problem-solving and decision-making. A board can't succeed if it functions on autopilot — or if its members treat the responsibility as a low priority.

There's one other time consideration: Investment markets don't care about what's convenient for a board. Financial opportunities (or risks) don't accommodate the busy personal schedules of board members. It's not surprising that so many struggle to find time to carry out their duties.

There's a third challenge...

3. The Financial Expertise Gap

As alluded to above, medical training, however rigorous, rarely includes a comprehensive financial education. As a result, while most board members are experts in complex medical procedures or cutting-edge healthcare research, few feel entirely comfortable discussing investment strategies, market dynamics, or portfolio theory.

Depending on the composition of a particular board, this expertise gap can show itself in a variety of ways:

- Unfamiliarity with certain financial terminology and concepts.
- Uncertainty when evaluating investment recommendations.
- Not knowing the best questions to ask financial advisors.
- Discomfort with risk assessment.
- Limited ability to judge investment performance.
- A natural tendency to focus on secondary issues that detract from the organization's primary goals.

Given enough time, intelligent medical professionals/board members could master complex financial concepts and skills. But as noted in challenge No. 2 above, "enough time" is the one thing busy board members don't have.

A final challenge many boards wrestle with is...

4. The Challenge of Continuity

In most organizations, the board's composition changes from year to year. This dynamic of people rotating into and out of leadership roles can create gaps in financial oversight and institutional knowledge.

New board members are like the "old" ones they're replacing. They typically possess varying amounts of financial expertise. What's more, experienced board members, in stepping down, often take institutional history and crucial financial context with them.

This is why so many nonprofit boards have difficulty in the following areas:

- Maintaining consistent investment strategies during board transitions.
- Preserving institutional knowledge about past financial decisions.
- Ensuring smooth handoffs of financial oversight responsibilities.
- Building and maintaining relationships with financial advisers.
- Implementing long-term financial planning initiatives.

A PATH FORWARD

These four challenges are significant. But they're not insurmountable. It's possible for nonprofit boards to:

- Develop a better understanding of the risks and returns of different investments.
- Build their financial knowledge systematically.
- Establish healthy financial guardrails for their organizations.
- Create sustainable oversight processes.
- Leverage professional expertise to their advantage.

Seeing your nonprofit experience those successes is what this book is all about. The goal is to help you become a more confident and effective steward of your organization's financial resources. That way, your organization can focus fully on its critical healthcare mission and be a catalyst for changed lives.

A FORMULA FOR SUCCESS

In working with hundreds of boards and board members, our team at MEDIQUS has developed a simple formula. It highlights the three areas that we believe nonprofit directors and boards need to prioritize when trying to guard, grow, and steward their organizations' investments.

That formula is:

Investment Consulting
+ Continuity Coordination
+ Ongoing Collaboration

Nonprofit Health!

Investment Consulting is about balancing **risk and return**: *Are the investments and the goals of our nonprofit carefully aligned?*

Continuity Coordination is about **organizational stability**: *Do we have clear systems in place to ensure that leadership transitions do not always lead to a total reset?*

Ongoing Collaboration refers to **communication and resources**: *Do we have the information and partners we need to navigate all kinds of situations?*

Over and over, we've seen that when boards focus on these three priorities, they are better positioned to lead their nonprofits to fiscal health, which allows them to have greater impact.

This book is arranged around that simple formula.

In Chapters 1–5, we'll get an overview of the critical issues facing nonprofit boards in the area of investment strategy. Chapters 6–8 will explore how boards can build leadership stability in their organizations. In chapters 9 and 10, we'll outline the practical issues involved in making sure your board has all the information and resources needed to lead your organization to mission success.

But before diving in, we should be clear on this: The goal of *When Mission Meets Money* isn't to turn you into a financial expert or give precise advice for handling your organization's investable assets.

Rather, the intent is to give you a broad framework, some basic knowledge, and practical tools so you and your colleagues can make informed decisions. In providing an overview of these subjects, we hope to help you answer the central question that all conscientious board members ask themselves in one way or another: "Are we doing the right things here?"

To demonstrate that these issues aren't merely hypothetical or theoretical, we'll begin each chapter with a fictional nonprofit and fictional characters wrestling with a common problem that can cause dire, real-world consequences. We take this approach to illustrate the challenges leaders face and provide potential solutions for navigating them. All these scenarios are loosely based on real-life examples that we've encountered in the nearly 30 years of advising nonprofit organizations.

But here's what's exciting: You and your colleagues will also have the opportunity to make a profound difference.

Just imagine how many lives you could impact for good.

PART ONE

Investment Consulting

+ Continuity Coordination

+ Ongoing Collaboration

Nonprofit Health!

CHAPTER 1

The Need for Guiding Principles

"Living without an aim is like sailing without a compass."

- John Ruskin, English writer, lecturer, historian

"Aileen, you got a second?"

Dr. Aileen McIntire, board chair of the National Association of Thoracic Surgeons, senses concern in her treasurer's voice. "Sure, David. What's up?"

"I'm looking at financial reports and ... well, I don't know how else to say it. It's bleak. Our portfolio is down 12% just this *quarter*. I got two panicky calls last night from board members basically saying, 'We need to shift everything to cash.'"

David is talking a mile a minute. "This board is *so* knee-jerk! Every one of our investment decisions over the last two years has been reactive." He sighs loudly, then continues. "Anyway, the bottom line isn't good. I'm worried!"

Aileen closes her eyes and leans back in her chair. She flashes back to the last board meeting. More than an hour of back-and-forth about investment options. A myriad of opinions. No decisions. Not a single one.

"We don't have a strategy," Aileen says quietly. "Not even a *semblance* of a strategy."

David nods. "We're totally driven by market swings. The board says it wants aggressive growth, but then, every time the market begins to drop, they all panic! Aileen, we're managing the Association's assets based on which board member talks the loudest and longest!"

"Meanwhile," Aileen adds, "No matter *what* the market does, we have to honor our grant commitments."

There's a pause.

Aileen continues, "We need some kind of agreed-upon framework for guiding our investment decisions."

"One hundred percent!" David says, "Last night — after those other calls — I talked to a friend who's on the board of a similar-sized nonprofit. *They don't have all this drama!* They've got some clear investment principles *in writing*!"

Aileen thinks about the stress of the last board meeting. She thinks about the group's ambitious grant program and the young researchers counting on their funding.

The conversation between Aileen and David highlights a common challenge for medical nonprofit boards: the lack of a clear, principled approach to investment management. Many simply don't have an agreed-upon strategy.

In this chapter, we will discuss the importance of creating investment guidelines that will support your organization's mission in light of a board member's heightened level of responsibility and the importance of an organization's assets. These concepts can then inform how you might develop an investment strategy that is based on more than just whatever "the market" is doing.

BUILDING AND MAINTAINING FINANCIAL SUSTAINABILITY

Why does every nonprofit need a clear, agreed-upon investment strategy? A strategy addresses two common reasons for financial missteps: panic and euphoria.

Panic, according to the Merriam-Webster Dictionary, is a sudden, overpowering fright — similar to the feelings exhibited in the opening scenario. Simply, it can feel like the sky is falling.

Euphoria, on the other hand, is a feeling of elation. Euphoria presents itself in a similar way, but from a more positive perspective. However, nothing moves in a smooth, straight, upward path. Recall the pre-dot-com bubble and the pre-COVID financial landscape. Things were nothing but good until they weren't.

Letting either or both of these emotions drive the investment decisions a nonprofit makes can have devastating effects. It is important to develop a strategy that continually keeps in mind the responsibility a nonprofit's leaders have and what a nonprofit's investments are ultimately meant to do.

Fundamentally, a nonprofit's strategy can start with the idea that its investments are meant to support the organization's long- and short-term financial obligations. The organization must have sufficient resources to fund current operations and future initiatives. That means protecting your organization's assets against financial risks and market volatility so they can support short-term needs, but also positioning them to grow so they can support future initiatives.

Growth is key if for no other reason than the impact of inflation. Warren Buffett famously said in 1977, "[t]he arithmetic makes it plain that inflation is a far more devastating tax than anything that has been enacted by our legislatures. The inflation tax has a fantastic ability to simply consume capital."[4] The value of a dollar today is not the same as the value of a dollar tomorrow, and while dollars may not experience decreases in value in a savings account or under a mattress, the erosion of value is still a very real risk.

Striking the right balance between growth and risk is difficult. Growth involves risk (e.g., volatility). It is a necessary tradeoff, but if not done thoughtfully, it can lead to panic when you feel like you "have to buy now" and euphoria when the investments feel like they can only increase in value.

In the end, having a strategy helps mitigate the impact of these two emotions and creates a framework you can follow in good times and bad.

However, in addition to this short and long-term balance, recall the importance of an organization's assets and the heightened level of responsibility as a fiduciary to the organization.

THE IMPORTANCE OF RESERVE FUNDS

We'll discuss reserve funds in more detail in Chapter 8, but for now, it's worth mentioning the importance of investable assets as a financial buffer for nonprofit organizations. Reserves are *not* about stockpiling wealth. They're about ensuring organizational resilience and mission continuity. They not only provide *stability*, but they also give organizations *flexibility* — a way to take advantage of strategic opportunities.

These monies have the ability to provide protection and create opportunity. A healthy "rainy day fund" serves as a safety net during unexpected challenges, such as economic downturns or public health crises. Think about the COVID-19 pandemic and its impact on the nonprofit industry. Reserves allow your organization to maintain critical services, honor commitments, and retain key staff when they're needed most.

But beyond mere survival, reserves enable your board to act decisively when opportunities arise, whether that means expanding services, investing in new technology, or responding to emerging community health needs.

A well-structured reserve fund can be beneficial in another way: It demonstrates responsible stewardship to donors and grant recipients, thereby enhancing organizational credibility. Ultimately, adequate reserves give your board the confidence to make strategic decisions without the constant strain of financial anxiety.

Since healthcare environments often change rapidly, when continuity of care is paramount, adequate reserves represent not just financial prudence but also a commitment to fulfilling the mission in good times and bad.

Creating and maintaining adequate reserves is one tangible way you can carry out your *fiduciary responsibility* as a board member.

WHAT IS A *FIDUCIARY*?

A *fiduciary* is someone who is legally and ethically bound to act for the benefit of another. Board members of nonprofits fall into this category. Your duty is to act solely for the benefit of the organization and its stakeholders (e.g., members).

How can you aim to fulfill this obligation? It's possible by consistently demonstrating three main actions:

1. **Care**. You exhibit reasonable and prudent skill and diligence in making decisions for your nonprofit.
2. **Loyalty**. You *always* act in the nonprofit's best interest. You *never* use your position with the organization to advantage yourself or others. This kind of integrity is vital to building and maintaining public trust in your organization.
3. **Obedience**. You work to achieve your nonprofit's mission, and you abide by all laws and regulations that govern it.

How do these functions look in day-to-day "real life"?

Care means being active and engaged. You attend meetings. You review reports closely and ask thoughtful questions. While you don't feel pressure to become an expert in all the issues that come before you, you do remain attentive and curious. When it comes to investment decisions, you're not overly aggressive. You wisely balance risk and return, sometimes giving risk more consideration and sometimes being more cautious.

Loyalty is reflected in how you answer questions like: Do I stand to receive a benefit, financial or otherwise, from a decision the board is considering? Do I own an asset in which the nonprofit is considering investing? Do I own interest in an entity the nonprofit might utilize? Would my perceived status among fellow members be enhanced by a certain decision? Identifying potential conflicts of interest and adhering to appropriate policy is essential.

Obedience means complying with all the policies that relate to your nonprofit's investments. This includes investment policies, spending policies, and reserve policies. In all your deliberations and actions, you adhere to these agreed-upon parameters.

These fiduciary guidelines aren't simply recommendations. They're mandatory. When a board doesn't function according to these standards, the consequences can be dire: reputational harm, a decline in donations, a loss of membership, lawsuits by donors or members, fines, even forfeiture of the organization's tax-exempt status. Individual board members can also be held personally liable if they are found to have acted recklessly.

To summarize: Serving on the board of a medical nonprofit is a great honor. It's an opportunity to do good in the world. But it's also a weighty responsibility that shouldn't be taken lightly. If you sometimes feel anxious in your role, you're not alone. But you don't want to exacerbate the stress by making investment decisions without the guidance of a clear strategy.

GUIDING PRINCIPLES FOR DEVELOPING AN INVESTMENT STRATEGY

We've covered the importance of an organization's assets, the importance of a strategy for managing those assets, and the responsibility individuals accept as leaders of an organization. But what are the steps necessary to develop an investment strategy?

After nearly 30 years of guiding organizations, MEDIQUS has identified three areas that we believe nonprofit organizations must address to create an investment strategy that allows them to maintain purchasing power in perpetuity, even as it supports their ongoing work:

1. The organization's **purpose** for its funds.
2. The organization's **objectives** (both short-term and long-term) for its funds.
3. The organization's **needs** from its funds.

We'll talk about these matters in greater detail in subsequent chapters. For now, here are a few specifics to illustrate these broad guiding principles.

Purpose

Determine the purpose of the funds by answering questions such as "Why do we have these funds?" or "What are these funds meant to do?" The answer, or answers, can inform how you should handle the funds from an investment standpoint.

For example, if funds are meant to be an extension of savings to support short-term operating expenses, then investing those in a higher-risk way would not be reasonable. If funds are meant to be a source of financial stability with no immediate need, then leaving them in a savings account may actually be a high-risk approach.

Understanding and regularly reaffirming the purpose of the funds you're overseeing provides the foundation for their investment.

Objectives

Consider how much the organization would like to see its invested funds grow and what degree of risk the organization is comfortable undertaking in order to accomplish that growth. For example, the organization may be focused on:

- A minimum return above the rate of inflation. This target allows for sustained (and even expanded) programming, even in the face of rising costs.
- Coverage of expenses. Your returns ideally are adequate to cover spending needs from the investments as well as all investment management fees, transaction costs, and administrative expenses so that you don't erode your principal.
- Risk parameters. Return and risk go hand-in-hand. Generally speaking, the greater return you seek, the greater risk you need

to be willing to take. But it's important to consider how much risk to take so that the investment of your organization's assets aligns with your organization's ability to endure volatility and comfort enduring it.

- Time horizon. Over what period of time should your strategy be tailored for? Is it the next 12 months? The next 12 years? The time horizon affects the acceptable level of risk. The longer the time horizon, all else equal, the greater the amount of risk that can be taken.

Needs

Finally, you want your strategy to consider your organization's needs from its investments, such as how much you may need to withdraw to support the operational costs of your nonprofit. This can establish a system whereby you have adequate funds for:

- Meeting regular daily expenses. This is cash available for day-to-day expenses and near-term obligations.
- Funding ongoing grants and initiatives. These dedicated reserves are held separately so the organization can honor commitments made to award recipients and grant programs.
- Handling emergency needs. These funds are held in reserve for unanticipated expenses or opportunities (e.g., short-term emergencies and long-term events like the COVID pandemic).

Even with this brief introduction, you can see how having a set of guiding principles is like having a financial North Star. An investment strategy based on clear, agreed-upon principles keeps a board from descending into reactive mode or being tempted to make impulsive decisions in the face of wild, temporary market swings (i.e., panic and euphoria).

With some guiding principles, you can stay on course and continue steering in the right direction when uncertainty inevitably spikes in the investment world. These principles serve not only as a compass, but they also provide accountability. With them, you can keep coming back to fundamental questions like: *Why are we doing what we're doing? What are these funds for? Is there alignment between our mission and the use of these funds? Are we comfortable with what we're seeing?*

In the next chapter, we'll turn to an age-old investment dilemma that every board faces: risk vs. reward.

PRACTICAL ACTION STEPS FOR BOARDS TO CONSIDER

1. **Create some written investment principles.** Begin developing a first-draft document of clear investment principles that align with your organization's mission. This document can provide a framework for decision-making and prevent reactive responses to temporary market changes.
2. **Embrace your fiduciary responsibility.** Fulfill your fiduciary duties of care, loyalty, and obedience by being actively engaged in financial decisions, avoiding conflicts of interest, and insisting on compliance with organizational policies and applicable laws.
3. **Establish distinct financial reserves.** Create a clear separation between funds designated for daily operations, ongoing grant commitments, or emergency needs to prepare for meeting organizational obligations, regardless of market conditions.
4. **Begin developing an investment strategy.** Create starting points for an investment policy considering the principles you've established, fiduciary responsibilities, and your organization's distinct financial assets. From there, you can better determine how to handle the more technical investment concepts (i.e., target returns, risk tolerance, etc.).

CHAPTER 2

Understanding Risk and Return

"The essence of investment management
is the management of risks,
not the management of returns. Well-managed
portfolios start with this precept."

- Benjamin Graham, *The Intelligent Investor*

Dr. Everett Tucker scans the faces on his computer screen. He's called this emergency meeting of the board of the American College of Neonatal Medicine because the organization's portfolio has dropped 21% in value in just over three months.

"Byron, thanks for joining us on such short notice." (Byron is the nonprofit's investment adviser.)

Byron nods. Dr. Tucker continues, "Folks, as I said in my email, due to the turmoil in the markets, we're close to falling below our minimum reserve requirements. So, I'll get straight to it. Do we want to stay the course with our current investment strategy? Or do we think it's time to be more conservative?"

Dr. Reena Ranjakar, a long-term board member and chair of pediatrics at a university hospital, speaks first. "Well, we *do* have three years of grant commitments to honor. And with everything going on, maybe we make changes and wait for things to settle down."

Heads bob up and down. There's some back and forth. One board member even calls for the group to become more aggressive so they can take advantage of down markets. The board member says they have done the same with their own investments, so the approach is reasonable here.

Byron clears his throat and asks Dr. Tucker for permission to share his screen. "Everyone, the investment climate right now is nerve-wracking. That's for sure. But if I may, I'd like to remind everyone that we discussed your risk tolerance at the end of last year.

"It was actually perfect timing. At that time, the markets were flat. As a result, nobody was feeling panicked... and no one was filled with irrational exuberance.

"You came out of that meeting with consensus. You said, 'When it comes to market volatility, our collective comfort level is here.' You can see on this slide that we were almost exactly in the middle of the risk-reward spectrum. Not overly risky, not overly conservative. And if we look back over the years, the group has been through periods like this before." Also, we walked through a number of factors to support the current strategy due to your risk tolerance."

There's silence while everyone scrutinizes the slide.

Byron takes a sip of water and continues, "Having said all that, I understand the concern. Contemplating *hypothetical* losses and facing *actual* losses are two very different things.

"Bottom line, I believe the strategy we've adopted is sound. We can certainly modify it if you wish, but my recommendation is to resist an overreaction."

Can you relate? Have you ever been in a meeting like that? Such scenarios are common in the nonprofit world when the markets become volatile.

The details, of course, vary from organization to organization. Still, the essential question remains: *How do we balance our desire for returns with our organization's ability and willingness to accept risk?*

Let's explore the issues nonprofit board members face when wrestling with this question.

THE TRADE-OFF

When it comes to investing, one of the most fundamental principles to understand is the relationship between risk and return. Simply put, risk refers to the possibility of losing some or all of the money you invest, while return is the potential gain or profit you expect to earn from your investment. These two elements are closely linked: Generally, the higher the potential return of an investment, the greater the risk involved.

This trade-off between risk and return is at the heart of every investment decision. Nonprofits must assess their own tolerance for risk and determine how much uncertainty they are willing to accept in pursuit of higher returns. For instance, stocks may offer high returns over time, but they also tend to fluctuate significantly in value. In contrast, bonds are typically more stable but offer lower returns.

Understanding the risk-return trade-off allows nonprofits to make informed decisions that best align their purpose, fiduciary responsibilities, financial goals, investment timeline, and comfort with uncertainty. By carefully balancing these factors, nonprofits can create a portfolio that strives to achieve an optimal mix of preservation and growth.

RETURN

An appropriate return objective can be based on the end goal for a given set of funds. For example, you want to see your reserves grow to X amount. Or perhaps you want to make sure your nonprofit's investments keep pace with inflation, spending, and costs. In this case, using an annualized return objective might be best.

Annualized is a similar concept to "average"; however, there is a critical distinction for purposes of return calculations. For example, if you have investments that are up 40% in one year, then down 50% the second year, and then up 10% in the third year, your average return would be 0%, and you would be even because 40 minus 50 plus 10 is 0, right?

Incorrect. Returns year-to-year are not independent of one another, which is what an annualized return incorporates. Based on the numbers provided, the annualized return is actually *negative,* because let's say you had $1 that grew to $1.40 (40% gain), then decreased in value by 50% to $0.70, then increased by 10% to $0.77. This illustrates the importance of appropriate reporting calculations and managing volatility.

Here are a few important questions to address when discussing growth targets:

1. *What's needed to maintain purchasing power?* Here, you want to calculate your required return by adding the inflation rate (maybe 2-3%), your spending rate (possibly 0-5%), and investment expenses (potentially up to as much as 1%). This total can represent your minimum target return.
2. *What other organizational assets and commitments are we managing?* Considering the nature of revenue, expenses, and other

assets that have been accumulated can be a good starting place for determining what return might be needed. Assessing how investment underperformance would affect your ability to maintain programs, grants, and operational stability can also be a prudent risk management strategy.

3. *Over what time horizon are we looking to achieve our investment objectives?* Define whether you're looking at 3–5 years for shorter-term goals or 10+ years for long-term sustainability. Various time horizons can require a range of risk/return trade-offs.

CHASING RETURNS

A common way to assess strategies is to reduce them to average rates of return. Every investor *loves* years like 2023 and 2024, when the markets do great. (If you've forgotten, the S&P 500 rose approximately 26.3% and 25% in those years, respectively.)

Every investor *dreads* years like 2022, when the markets "take a beating." (For context, the S&P 500 dropped 18.1% that year, and was down about 24% over the first nine months before a strong rally in the fourth quarter.)

Unfortunately, since no investor has a crystal ball or time machine, we can never know in advance what's ahead. We're always bumping up against this ever-present reality of risk versus return.

In bull markets, we don't think much about risk. Everyone just wants to capitalize on all that growth! In such times, it's common for organizations with diversified portfolios — and returns that aren't as eye-popping — to start fidgeting. They wonder whether they might be better off moving their investments into whatever category has been generating the most glowing returns.

The thinking usually goes like this: "Sure, there might be more risk and volatility. But over the long haul, look at that average annual gain! Forget the downturns. Let's focus on the upside!"

But reducing an investment strategy to "we only go with the highest historic averages" ignores what happens during times of economic turmoil.

What about events like the crash of 2008-2009 or the onset of a global pandemic in 2020? Is confidence in a long-term average enough during big downturns? Or does strong emotion generated by a steep and sudden decline take over when the decreases in value are in real time to the assets you are overseeing?

Also, just because a particular investment or category has been the best performer does not mean it will remain so. The investment world's famous disclosure is "past performance is not indicative of future results."

COSTS

Costs have been mentioned a few times for determining target rates of return. But what might costs include? It is critical to understand costs and their structures because the higher your costs, the higher the hurdles your investments must overcome in order to grow.

Costs may include any or all of the following:

- Management fees (e.g., adviser compensation): The direct cost of professional investment management, this is typically a percentage of assets under management (AUM).
- Internal expenses (e.g., mutual fund or exchange-traded fund costs): The ongoing operational costs of investment vehicles can significantly affect your long-term returns.
- Administrative costs (e.g., custodian fees): These are charges for holding and safeguarding assets, processing transactions, and providing statements and tax documents.
- Trading/strategy costs (e.g., commissions, bid-ask spreads): These are the visible and sometimes hidden costs of buying and selling securities, including the difference between purchase and sale prices.
- Hidden costs (e.g., opportunity/delay costs from the timing of buying and selling): These less-obvious costs include the market impact of trades, timing delays, and missed opportunities due to prolonged investment decisions.

Knowing what management fee or internal expenses your nonprofit pays is one part of the analysis, but understanding the structure and how the ongoing strategy can affect all costs is even more important.

USE OF BENCHMARKS

If your organization establishes a target return, you'll likely want to use a benchmark to ensure the results you actually see are reasonable. It's common for boards to ask, "How do our returns compare to how the S&P 500 is doing?" While this question is understandable, it can lead to an inaccurate perspective and potentially prompt inappropriate action.

Consider three reasons the S&P 500's status isn't always relevant:

1. The S&P 500 is only one equity index. It tracks 500 of the largest U.S. companies. Your nonprofit likely owns (or should own) a broader blend of investments.
2. Different investments offer different risk characteristics. For example, bonds have predetermined features while stocks have unknown variables.
3. A nonprofit's investment strategy needs to account for current and future beneficiaries' needs, which often requires different types of investments. In short, the S&P index (or any single index) may not align with your nonprofit's objectives.

Benchmarks are helpful tools, but without thoughtful selection, they can lead to unreasonable expectations, performance chasing, or an inappropriate strategy.

What about risk?

THE RISK REALITY

Risk (i.e., the possible fluctuation in value over a given time period) isn't so fun to ponder. However, it is arguably the more important aspect in determining an investment strategy because, all else equal, investors generally feel more pain from losses than joy from gains. Risk can (and should) be viewed in two ways:

1. **Your *ability* to take risks.**

   A nonprofit's ability to take risks is based on multiple objective factors. Let's put them in the form of questions:

   - *How many months of operating expenses are in your checking/savings?* This can be your immediate safety net, your first line of defense against market downturns and expenses that come out of nowhere. In our experience, most medical nonprofits elect to keep 3–6 months in a highly liquid account. The less you have here, all else equal, the lower your ability to take risks, as you have less buffer before needing to access invested funds.

- *How many months of operating expenses do you have in investments?* This represents your longer-term financial cushion, typically targeting at least 12 months of total reserves when combined with checking/savings. The more held in investments, the greater the ability to take risks, as there is more cushion to absorb fluctuations in value.
- *What are your nonprofit's sources of revenue?* Understanding whether you rely on grants, donations, program fees, or endowment income helps determine how much risk you can afford to take with your organization's investments. If there is a single source of revenue that can vary year-to-year, this could lead to a lesser ability to take risks because of the uncertainty in revenue.
- *How many sources of revenue are there?* Diversification of revenue sources can provide stability. Having a variety of funding streams often means that you can take more risk with your investments.
- *Is there a minimum amount your organization aims to hold per its policies?* Your organization's policy requirements may create a floor below which you desire not to fall. For your organization, this can directly affect the level of investment risk that is appropriate. For example, if an organization has a policy to maintain a minimum of six months of expenses in long-term reserves, and the group has seven months of funds available, then it may consider a more conservative approach than if it had 12 months of expenses available.
- *What near-term spending do you need (or plan to do) from investments?* Anticipated withdrawals for programs, grants, or operations should be factored into your risk ability. The more regular and sizeable the withdrawals, the more conservative you may need to be. However, a planned spending amount that fits relative to return objectives may require taking additional risk.

2. **Your *Willingness* to Take Risk**

   This is more subjective, as it is influenced by factors such as emotion, psychology, and a board's "personality." Again, we'll put these considerations in the form of questions:

   - *What amount of decrease could you face without losing sleep?* This isn't just about numbers. It's about comfort. It's about your board's collective comfort level with watching account values decline. Having this kind of advanced self-awareness (and investing accordingly) can help guard against panicked, reactive decisions.

- *Do board members differentiate between risk to the organization's investments and the risks they willingly incur with personal investments?* It's imperative for board members to separate their personal risk tolerance from what's appropriate for their organization's mission and stakeholders. What someone may feel comfortable doing with their own finances may be quite different than what is best for an organization.
- *How might this "willingness" change as leadership changes?* New board members bring different perspectives and introduce a variety of risk tolerances. For this reason, it's wise to regularly review and reaffirm your organization's investment strategies. Given the turnover that can occur, the factors affecting an organization's ability to take risks play an even more important role because there are clear metrics new board members can reference for understanding why the organization invests the way that it does.

How you can best balance these two major concepts brings us to asset allocation.

THE IMPORTANCE OF ASSET ALLOCATION

Asset allocation is the practice of balancing your portfolio by investing in a variety of asset classes, such as stocks, bonds, and cash. Each component is designed to provide certain benefits for your portfolio and, ideally, help mitigate the risks of the other components.

Stocks or equities offer the potential to earn attractive returns, but they entail more risk than some other types of investments. Bonds can be an integral part of asset allocation because they generally provide more stability than equities. Cash assets, such as money markets, offer liquidity and a convenient "parking place" for cash intended for upcoming investment opportunities. By including all of these, and possibly more, in your portfolio, you balance the risk and return across various categories.

Within these general classes, there are sub-categories. For example, the equity class of assets can be further divided into U.S. large company stocks, U.S. small company stocks, and the stocks of international companies. Fixed-income vehicles can be subcategorized by length of maturity and include both U.S. and international bonds.

Over time, these asset classes perform differently. This performance difference applies to international stocks and bonds as well. Therefore, diversification among different asset classes is an important way to maintain a more consistent level of performance over time.

MODERN PORTFOLIO THEORY

Another important concept in the asset allocation process is *modern portfolio theory*. Three economists were awarded the 1990 Nobel Prize in Economics for their work in developing this theory, which has to do with the efficient management of an investment portfolio. Three basic premises of modern portfolio theory are worth considering.

First, markets are efficient. It is difficult for an individual investor to consistently beat the market over time. Technology has created an environment where information is instantly available to potentially limitless numbers of investors.

Second, attention should be focused on the investment portfolio as a whole rather than on individual investments. Studies have shown that *over 90% of the impact of an investment portfolio is a result of the selection of asset classes rather than the selection of a particular security or market timing.*[5] Therefore, much of the energy spent trying to pick or time the purchase of the "best" stock, bond, or mutual fund is wasted. Individual investors may be much better off identifying and monitoring a specific asset class selection among domestic and international asset classes.

Third, at any given level of risk, there is a particular combination of asset classes that will maximize return. For example, let's say your investments have 60% in stocks, 30% in bonds, and 10% in cash, and an alternative portfolio has 60% in stocks and 40% in bonds. Each had the same rate of return over the last five years, but the alternative portfolio saw lower decreases in value when declines occurred. This means the alternative is the more efficient of the two — the same return for less risk. Therefore, not only is the selection of the asset class important, but also determining the amount to be invested in each class will help optimize returns at a given level of risk.

It is also worth noting that the terms "stocks" and "bonds" can include an enormous number of different possibilities. You can have stocks of companies in the United States or companies outside of the United States, large companies or small companies, companies in particular sectors (technology, energy, real estate), or companies of particular models (i.e., value versus growth). Similar differentiation can occur with bonds, too. So it may seem simple to say "We'll follow a 60/40 allocation" (60% of an account being invested in companies and 40% being invested in bonds), but there is a lot more to the decision when you have to consider what will make up the 60 and 40, respectively.

In the end, the risk-return question is about balance, and it requires accepting some degree of uncertainty. How you determine the degree of uncertainty can depend on many factors. This is because the process is partly based on "what-ifs" going forward, not just what has happened in the past.

PRACTICAL ACTION STEPS FOR BOARDS TO CONSIDER

1. **Complete a risk capacity analysis**. Conduct a thorough assessment of your organization's ability and willingness to take risk and how that fits with the returns you seek.
2. **Document your return objectives and risk tolerance metrics**. Establish specific, measurable risk parameters that align with your organization's investment ability and investment willingness levels.
3. **Align your investment strategy with your risk tolerance**. Ensure your portfolio matches your documented risk profile.
4. **Establish a regular review process**. Create a schedule for monitoring and adjusting risk management strategies.

CHAPTER 3

Understanding Types of Investments

"[Portfolio management is] a very special problem in engineering, of determining the most reliable and efficient way of reaching a specified goal, given a set of policy constraints, and working within a remarkably uncertain, probabilistic, always changing world of partial information and misinformation, all filtered through the inexact prism of human interpretation."

–Charles D. Ellis, *Investment Policy: How to Win the Loser's Game*

Members of the finance committee of The Brenner Foundation for Children's Health are discussing whether they should move the non-profit's reserve funds to some different investments.

Frustration is growing. It's not quite an argument, but there are strong and diverse opinions about how to both protect and grow the organization's $7.8 million portfolio.

Dr. Mario Scarpelli mentions "three AI stocks with the potential to be the next NVIDIA. Imagine tripling our money in the next couple of years! Why don't we put at least some of our reserve funds in a few stocks like that?"

"Because we're not running a day trading account," Dr. Kelley Hackman interrupts. "Our strategy needs to reflect our long-term mission. I think we…"

Dr. Michael O'Connor throws up his hands and cuts her off. "Just put it all in an S&P 500 index fund and be done with it! It's simple, straightforward, and proven. Doesn't the S&P have, like, a 10% average annual return over the last 60 years?"

Dr. Emily Crow, the esteemed researcher, author, and children's health advocate, pushes her wire-rimmed glasses up her nose and wrinkles her brow. "That's true, Mike. But that's an *average*. You occasionally have years like 2022, when it's down significantly. I say we go heavier into bonds. I know they're not 'sexy.' But they're safe. Or, at least, safe-ER."

There's audible grumbling and groaning, prompting the organization's executive director to speak up. Erika Hartnett has led three nonprofits over the last 28 years. This isn't her first investment discussion rodeo.

"I appreciate the various perspectives. To be honest, I wasn't anticipating such a lively discussion. But I know that's only because we all recognize that what we're doing here is bigger than numbers on a spreadsheet. We're trying to improve healthcare for kids. And, obviously, if we can grow our resources, that will allow us to do so much more.

"So, I'm glad we have our financial adviser on this call. Sarah, walk us through our options again. What are the pros and cons of the various investment vehicles available to us? Remind us how each aligns — or doesn't — with our mission, our short- and long-term goals, and our collective comfort level."

Sarah Pendergrass smiles. "I'd be glad to do that."

The goal of the next few pages is to briefly explore the most common types of investments for medical nonprofits.

Much as Sarah did with the Brenner Foundation finance team, we'll quickly highlight the basic advantages, disadvantages, and strategic applications of each. Specifically, we'll look at:

- Common asset classes (stocks and bonds).
- Common vehicles for owning traditional investments (mutual funds, exchange-traded funds).
- Alternative investments.
- Some practical risk management considerations.
- The importance of evaluating all these options through the lens of organizational needs, mission alignment, and long-term sustainability.

"LOANER-SHIP" VS. OWNERSHIP

At the risk of oversimplifying, we could say that investment vehicles generally fall into two fundamental types: "loaner-ship" assets and ownership assets.

"Loaner-ship" Assets

Also commonly referred to as fixed income or cash equivalents, these represent short-term loans made to an entity in exchange for:

- A promised interest rate. The borrower commits to paying you a specific percentage return on your investment, providing predictable income streams for your nonprofit.
- Repayment of the principal after an agreed-upon period. Your original investment amount is returned at maturity, allowing for precise financial planning.

Common examples include money market funds, short-term government and corporate bonds, certificates of deposit (CDs), and Treasury bills.

On the plus side, these investments:

- *Offer high liquidity.* You can access these funds quickly, making them ideal for operating expenses and emergency funds. Most can be converted to cash within a few days. This availability makes them useful for managing your nonprofit's cash flow.
- *Tend to be certain in value.* Bank money markets are FDIC-insured; mutual fund money markets typically offer higher yields but are not FDIC-insured. This trade-off requires careful consideration of your organization's risk tolerance.

On the negative side, because these investments come with lower risk, *they can result in lower returns.* And if inflation exceeds their yield, they lose their purchasing power.

Think of "loaner-ship" assets this way: The investor (whether an individual or an organization) functions like a bank, loaning assets and collecting interest on the loan.

Bonds

Bonds are a type of loaner-ship asset. They represent the debt of a government, municipality, or corporation. Most bonds are issued in $1,000 units, which helps investors with portfolio planning and diversification.

The interest rates offered depend on the creditworthiness of the issuer and the maturity length.

- Better-rated issuers typically pay lower rates; those with lower credit quality generally offer higher interest rates. This fundamental relationship between risk and reward (see Chapter 2) helps boards evaluate whether higher yields justify the increased risk.
- Higher yields are typically offered on bonds with longer terms to compensate for the relatively lower level of liquidity.

It's important to note the types of risk bonds can have. One element of risk with bonds is interest rate risk. Interest rate risk is the possibility of a loss in value due to a change in market interest rates. In short, as interest rates rise, bond prices fall. This inverse relationship affects the market value of your holdings, although holding bonds to maturity eliminates this risk.

However, it would be an oversimplification to think of interest rates in a singular way. No single interest rate affects all fixed income. As mentioned earlier, interest rates can vary based on the amount of time until they mature (related to a concept called "the yield curve"). For example, a bond that matures in 20 years likely has a different interest rate than a bond that matures in two years. These bonds are affected not by a single interest rate but by interest rates associated with their maturity.

So, when you hear that interest rates are rising or falling, it's important to determine which interest rates are being referred to. For example, let's say you buy bonds in anticipation of the Federal Reserve decreasing interest rates. The interest rate the Federal Reserve can more directly affect is the Federal Funds Rate, an interest rate banks charge one another for overnight (very short-term) lending. This interest rate can affect other interest rates, but the longer the maturity, the less impact the Federal Funds Rate will have.

Back to our example, the Federal Reserve does, in fact, decrease this overnight lending rate, but you bought long-term, 20-year bonds. As a result, you may not see the price increase you expected because long-term 20-year interest rates did not automatically decrease as well.

Furthermore, long-term bonds are often associated with higher levels of volatility. This is because longer-term bonds are determined more by economic and market factors, and a lot can happen between now and the date of maturity, which will affect a bond's value.

Another element of risk associated with fixed income is credit risk. Credit risk is the risk of losses due to a borrower failing to make timely and full payments of interest or principal. In other words, you loan your money to someone, but they don't pay you back. All else equal, the less creditworthy a borrower, the higher the interest rate they pay you to borrow money in order to compensate for the risk that they may not repay you.

Sometimes, a fixed-income portfolio is put together based on picking the highest interest rates. However, this may create a higher risk because the higher interest rate may reflect a less creditworthy borrower.

These uncertainties can increase volatility in a fixed-income portfolio, so it is important to understand the interest rates, maturity structures, and credit quality, among other factors, of the bonds your organization chooses to own.

Ownership Assets

Ownership assets represent actual ownership in a company or enterprise. The value of your share in ownership is tied directly to the enterprise's value. Your investment's worth fluctuates based on market perception, expectations, and actual business performance. These factors and the potentially endless number that influence them often lead to both greater risk and higher potential reward.

Examples of ownership assets include individual stocks, real estate, and "hard assets" like gold. Each of these assets responds differently to market conditions, providing various ways to diversify, grow, and protect your nonprofit's portfolio.

Equity Investments

Let's start with a brief overview of equity investments and key features:

Common Stock. Buying stock in a company gives an individual or organization ownership in that entity. This means:

- Your investment grows or lessens as the company's stock appreciates or decreases in value. Consequently, your investment value can increase substantially.
- You may receive dividends, although it isn't guaranteed. These regular payments can provide income, although companies often reduce or eliminate them in difficult economic times.
- You receive voting rights in company decisions. This ownership privilege allows you to influence corporate governance, although the impact depends on the size of your holding.
- Your total return is a combination of the stock's appreciation plus whatever dividends you receive.

Size. "Size" refers to the total value of the company determined in the stock market. Companies can be considered large, mid-sized, or small. Each has its own return and risk features, so how your organization weights the companies it owns based on size can have a meaningful impact on the results that you see.

Style. "Style" refers to the approach or strategy used to select stocks, based on characteristics such as growth potential, valuation, or a combination of both. The strategy helps categorize investment strategies based on how they aim to generate returns by focusing on a particular style or mix.

- Growth style focuses on companies with strong earnings growth potential, often regardless of current valuation. These companies are expected to grow earnings or revenues faster than the market average. Companies in the technology industry have been commonly associated with this style.
- Value style focuses on companies that appear undervalued based on financial metrics such as earnings, dividends, or book value.

Each style can go through periods of over- and underperformance relative to one another and to broad benchmarks. Understanding whether there is, or you intend to have, a style focus is important to best understand your investment strategy.

Sectors. Stocks can be categorized by a company's economic activity. For example, companies might be categorized as a technology company (software, semiconductors, IT services), an energy company (oil and gas producers), a consumer discretionary company (retail, auto, luxury goods), or many others. Companies across sectors can be affected by various economic variables to varying degrees.

If your organization focuses on sectors, it's important to understand how it invests in the sectors and the various risks associated with those sectors.

International Equities. Investing in foreign companies can provide geographical diversification, but this includes taking on specific risks:

- Currency fluctuations and exchange rates can affect your returns positively or negatively.
- Investing in other countries includes the risks caused by political turmoil and economic instability in global markets.

These factors, while never predictable, do call for careful consideration.

Real Estate. A real estate investment creates ownership in real property. It can be a purchase of a medical office building, brick-and-mortar retail store, house, apartment building, or other property. You can purchase real estate individually as well as through investment vehicles, which we'll cover in a little more detail later.

Real estate acts similarly to both stock and bonds, so it's often considered a hybrid, or alternative, investment category. The appreciation potential of the physical property is similar to that of stocks. The unknown timeline and cash flows that real estate can produce also make it a comparable investment to stocks. The cash flows also make it similar to bonds. The rent payments properties collect are similar to bonds' interest payments. The term of leases creates a situation where payments are relatively more certain as well.

Due to the hybrid nature, the risks of stocks and bonds apply to real estate as well. So, depending on a given market environment, you could see fluctuations similar to stocks. And interest rate changes and creditworthiness could affect real estate investments just as they would affect bonds. So, while real estate is a way to diversify your nonprofit's investments, that doesn't mean you'll see vastly different outcomes than the other areas your nonprofit has already invested in.

Commodities. Commodities are other real assets in which you can invest. Common examples are precious metals, industrial metals, agricultural products, and energy products. You can invest by actually owning these assets (think bars of gold), but more commonly, these are owned by way of derivatives contracts (i.e., futures or forwards contracts). These contracts allow an investor to participate in a commodity's investment market without actually owning and storing the physical asset.

Commodities can provide additional diversification beyond more traditional asset classes such as stocks and bonds. They are commonly associated with inflation protection due to the theoretical idea that as prices increase, the cost of a commodity investment will as well.

And while often thought of as a way to enhance downside protection (i.e., gold as a store-of-value), they may result in higher levels of risk for a few reasons. As a store-of-value, their value is driven by the supply and demand of what you, I, or the person next to us believes the commodity is worth. Traditional economic factors, such as economic growth, can result in fluctuations in value. Other factors, like weather or natural disasters, can also play a role in creating more volatility. Liquidity can vary depending on how you own a given commodity. And if you own commodities via derivatives, the ability of the other party to the contract to honor the contract can be a risk, and you inherently create a leveraged investment because, in a derivative contract, you pay a premium for the contract but not the full amount of what the underlying asset is worth.

INVESTMENT VEHICLES

So, we've covered the various types of investments your nonprofit can use. But how does your nonprofit go about owning them? Below are a few of the ways you can purchase these various investments other than owning them individually.

Mutual Funds

A mutual fund pools money from many investors to purchase a diversified portfolio of stocks, bonds, or other securities. The fund is professionally managed in accordance with specific investment objectives.

Pros:

- Financial professionals/fund managers handle investment decisions.
- Can receive diversification across many securities with a relatively low amount invested.
- Available in a wide variety to match different goals.
- Simple to purchase.
- Dividends and capital gains can be automatically reinvested.

Cons:

- Fund performance can be contingent on the manager's skill.
- Management fees can reduce returns.
- Only trades at the end of the day (at a set price) after the markets close.
- Most have minimum investment requirements (often $1,000–$3,000).

Exchange-Traded Funds

ETFs are similar to mutual funds in that they also pool investor money to buy a diversified portfolio; however, ETFs trade on exchanges like individual stocks throughout the day, meaning their trade price can fluctuate during the day.

Pros:

- Generally offer lower fees than comparable mutual funds.
- Trade throughout the day at changing market prices.
- Usually no minimum investment beyond one share.
- Many track specific indexes with transparent holdings.

Cons:

- Trading requires a brokerage account.
- Bid-ask spreads can add costs when trading.
- Some niche ETFs have higher fees.
- May not offer automatic dividend reinvestment.
- Can trade at prices slightly different from their underlying value.

Real Estate Investment Trusts

REITs are publicly traded stocks that invest in commercial property. Benefits of REITs include:

- Ninety percent of earnings must be paid out to investors as dividends: This requirement often results in a higher yield than that earned by traditional stocks.
- The opportunity to benefit from real estate investing without having to get involved in direct property management and the hassles of direct ownership.
- Better investment performance when interest rates fall, and occupancy rates rise. This is a fairly reliable indicator of REIT performance.
- This investment vehicle offers potential for both regular income and appreciation of the value of your portfolio.

RISK MANAGEMENT THROUGH DIVERSIFICATION

It's vital to remember that no single investment or vehicle is ideal for every nonprofit or all situations. A nonprofit has various interests for its investments: short- and long-term support, current and future obligations. Therefore, you probably don't want to try to find the proverbial needle in the haystack. You want to buy the haystack. You want lots of different needles!

In other words, broad yet careful participation in the markets — i.e., putting your eggs in multiple baskets — is often the wise course of action. How exactly you do that goes back to the principles we discussed in Chapter 1 and the risk and return concepts addressed in Chapter 2.

This is true for several reasons:

- Different asset classes often (not always) perform differently as market conditions change. This fact is a good thing. It means you and your board can build a portfolio that offers both risk protection *and* growth opportunities.

- When your investments are diversified, you may see certain vehicles lose value while others grow. That's okay. While you may not see the same highs as the best performing investments, you also won't see the full extent of the lows from the worst performing investments.
- Your nonprofit's unique needs should always drive your board's allocation decisions. How you invest should correspond with your immediate operational needs and your long-term objectives.

- By conducting regular reviews and rebalancing your portfolio, you can maintain desired risk levels and keep your nonprofit on a good financial track.

PUTTING IT ALL TOGETHER

How do all these options possibly come together to make an investment strategy? The earlier discussions about purpose, objectives, risk and return, needs, etc., are so important. They should help guide how much you invest in areas like stocks versus bonds or alternative categories. They should guide what types of products you consider for making such investments (i.e., individual stocks/bonds versus exchange-traded funds). And they inform how you can manage the risks inherent in each of these categories and vehicles, so that, in the end, you can establish an approach that balances the issues Charles Ellis mentioned in the opening quote.

PRACTICAL ACTION STEPS FOR BOARDS TO CONSIDER

1. **Assess your organization's specific needs**, including growth and income requirements, time horizon, and risk tolerance, before making investment decisions.
2. **Consider diversification** across multiple investment vehicles rather than concentrating in a single asset type.
3. **Evaluate the different types of investments** between "loaner-ship" assets (e.g., bonds, CDs) for stability and "ownership" assets (e.g., stocks, REITs, etc.) for growth potential.
4. **Explore various investment vehicles** as a way to gain diversified exposure without selecting individual securities.
5. **Bring everything together** in a manner that fits your organization's purpose for its funds, return goals, risk tolerance, time horizon, and needs.

CHAPTER 4

Socially Conscious Investing

"It's easy to make a buck. It's a lot tougher to make a difference."

- Tom Brokaw, American journalist and author

In July 2024, the Lung Health Association (LHA) faced an unexpected PR crisis.

Several conscientious stakeholders discovered the nonprofit's investment portfolio included significant holdings in two companies that were heavily involved in tobacco products. LHA board members found themselves struggling to explain to association members why an organization dedicated to lung health owned stock in corporations that were arguably contradictory to the organization's purpose.

This situation highlights the kinds of questions many nonprofit boards face today:

- Should we be investing in companies that harm the environment?
- What about industries that exploit their workers or companies that turn a blind eye to human rights violations in the countries where they operate?
- Is it hypocritical for a medical nonprofit to invest in companies that sell products that pose a danger to individual and public health (e.g., alcohol stocks, tobacco companies, or firearm manufacturers)?
- Is it possible for a nonprofit to be values-conscious in its investing and still support the organization's goals?

UNDERSTANDING ESG INVESTING

People speak of ESG (environmental, social, and governance) investing, values-based investing, ethical investing, socially conscious investing, and impact investing. While there *are* technical differences among these various terms, they are often used interchangeably. Generally speaking, people use these terms to convey the idea of "We want our investments to (1) make a profit, but also (2) *make the world a better place.*

The ESG approach involves ensuring an organization's investments are aligned with the values of the group. Some would explain, "It's our way of distancing ourselves from objectionable products or services." Others would describe it as "an effort to support the causes and/or principles our organization is meant to enhance."

It can become a tricky topic, though. Boards are made up of people. People have their own perspectives and beliefs. What's considered "good" or "acceptable" practices can vary from one person to another. A board member from Texas may have a different perspective than a board member from California about investing in energy companies.

Or, if ESG ratings or scores are used, can you make apples-to-apples assessments? One ESG score may reflect poorly on a company, while a score from another rating system may be favorable.

Even if leadership can agree on a set of criteria around ESG investing, where do they draw the line? You may determine you will exclude companies that sell alcohol, but if a top-five Fortune 500 company owns grocery stores that sell alcohol, does that mean you must exclude that company from your nonprofit's portfolio?

These are not easy questions to answer, so it may help to have some guidelines. When considering socially conscious investing, boards must first establish clear parameters that reflect their organization's values and mission. These parameters typically encompass four key areas:

1. The purpose and objectives of the organization's funds.
2. Specific concerns or causes to address.
3. The organization's investment approach.
4. Implementation thresholds.

Let's look at each of those areas in more detail…

The foundation of any socially conscious investment strategy begins with understanding the purpose and objectives of your organization's funds. This means identifying both your short-term operational needs and your long-term strategic goals. For medical nonprofits, this requires balancing the need to fund current, ongoing programs while ensuring sustainable growth for future initiatives. Without such balance, the organization may go down roads and take risks that leave the investments unable to fulfill their fundamental purpose.

Organizations must also identify any specific issues they wish to address through their investment strategy. Since personal beliefs, values, and preferences can lead to endless discussions, it may help to focus on issues that are more directly related to the organization's mission. For example, a medical society focused on lung health might choose to avoid investments in tobacco companies, as companies in that industry are more directly in conflict with lung health. This can hopefully keep the scope of the discussion focused as opposed to going into every board member's personal beliefs.

The manner in which a board addresses these concerns can take either a direct or an indirect investment approach. Direct investment exposure refers to owning shares in companies that produce controversial products. Indirect exposure might involve investments in companies that distribute or sell such products. Given how diversified companies can be these days, boards should consider whether to exclude both types of exposure or focus only on direct involvement.

Finally, ideally, organizations can establish specific thresholds and limits. This involves determining acceptable percentages of portfolio exposure to certain industries, products, or activities. It might also require using ESG scoring requirements to evaluate potential investments. This way, you can incorporate guidelines for current and future boards to follow, while allowing some flexibility in the process. Again, you may end up handcuffing your organization if you try to address every type of company that may possibly be contrary to your organization's mission, given the diversification companies have in their business models.

UNDERSTANDING THE TRADEOFFS

Socially conscious investing offers benefits, but it also involves important considerations. The primary advantage is the opportunity to align an organization's values with its investment decisions. This has the potential to strengthen stakeholder trust and preserve organizational integrity. For medical nonprofits, this alignment can be particularly powerful, demonstrating consistency between a group's mission and its financial practices.

However, boards need to weigh several potential challenges carefully. Socially conscious investing might limit diversification opportunities. By excluding certain sectors or profitable companies from a nonprofit's investment universe, the growth needed to support the organization's ultimate goals may be absent.

In addition, a concentration on a few companies that focus on doing good in a handful of areas can potentially increase the risk to an organization's portfolio. Additionally, values-based funds may incur higher administrative costs due to the increased research and screening requirements.

One other consideration is the lack of standardization in ESG metrics and reporting. The various rating agencies sometimes evaluate the same company differently, making it challenging to ensure the consistent application of ESG criteria. This inconsistency in standards requires due diligence.

IMPLEMENTATION STRATEGIES

Successful implementation of an ESG investment strategy requires a systematic approach. Organizations can use various screening methods, from excluding specific industries (negative screening) to actively seeking companies with positive environmental or social impacts (positive screening).

Some organizations opt for a hybrid approach, combining both methods to create a well-rounded portfolio that reflects their values while maintaining financial performance. An experienced professional can help you navigate the complexities of socially conscious investing, from identifying appropriate screening criteria to selecting suitable investment vehicles. They can also assist in monitoring portfolio performance to ensure that any ESG investments continue to meet both financial and social objectives.

IS SOCIALLY CONSCIOUS INVESTING RIGHT FOR YOUR NONPROFIT?

Socially conscious investing offers an opportunity (or a challenge) for nonprofit boards to align their investment strategies with their organizational values while maintaining financial health and stability.

Doing it productively requires careful consideration of parameters, a clear understanding of the tradeoffs, and systematic implementation with professional guidance. The good news? By taking a thoughtful, measured approach to socially conscious investing, boards can better position themselves to implement strategies that serve both their financial needs and the broader mission of benefiting society — and hopefully avoid the kind of PR nightmare that the Lung Health Association endured in 2024.

In Part 2, we'll discuss three documents that can give your nonprofit board greater clarity and more continuity in the face of inevitable change.

PRACTICAL ACTION STEPS FOR BOARDS TO CONSIDER

If your board is considering implementing a socially conscious/ESG investment strategy, several key actions can make the process easier.

1. **Create a clear set of written guidelines** that spell out your investing criteria and what values best support your mission. These guidelines might include specific metrics and thresholds for evaluating potential investments.
2. **Develop a process for regular review and updates of your ESG criteria and performance.** Since markets and social issues change and evolve, your investment strategy should adapt accordingly.
3. **Be transparent in your communication with stakeholders** about your values-based investment approach and how it might impact financial performance. This transparency will help maintain trust and support for your strategy.
4. **Maintain a clear focus on your fiduciary responsibility.** While your values are critical, they should never be divorced from the financial metrics necessary to ensure sustainable long-term performance for your nonprofit.

PART TWO

Investment Consulting

+ Continuity Coordination

+ Ongoing Collaboration

Nonprofit Health!

CHAPTER 5

Investment Policy Statements

"The best shield for long-term policies against the outrageous attacks of acute short-term data and distress are knowledge and understanding committed to writing."

— Charles D. Ellis, *Investment Policy: How to Win the Loser's Game*

At an Association for Spina Bifida Research board meeting, the conversation turns to investments. The organization has grown steadily. Its investments are mainly reserves that ideally can one day help support key organizational initiatives. ASBR has focused on bonds and some stock funds based on prior board members' experience and suggestions.

Dr. Smith, a respected physician and new board member, leans forward. "We're being too conservative. If we want to grow these funds to support our initiatives, we need to be more aggressive. There's a biotech stock I've seen that's done really well — great returns, little risk. I can reallocate some of our portfolio and get us better performance. I'm happy to handle it myself."

A few heads nod. Dr. Smith is clearly sharp and committed to the mission. But one board member, Dr. Wickman, speaks up.

"Thanks, Dr. Smith. But if you're managing the investments, how would ongoing monitoring work? Would you give updates? What if things don't go well with this biotech investment? And what happens when you're no longer on the board?"

Dr. Smith shrugs, "It's pretty standard. Once I set it up, we could shift it back to a 60/40 stocks-to-bonds mix if things go sideways — everyone does that. It'll take care of itself."

The room goes quiet. It sounded simple enough and appealing despite the questions about who would actually be responsible, or how "everyone does that" would work for them.

This scenario underscores a fundamental tenet: Having an investment policy is critical. An investment policy ensures that investment decisions aren't dependent on any one person, defines who can make those decisions, and establishes a consistent strategy current *and* future boards can follow that is aligned with the nonprofit's mission and goals, rather than "general market" practices.

But what goes into an investment policy? And how might you create one?

WHAT IS AN INVESTMENT POLICY STATEMENT?

An investment policy statement (IPS) is a comprehensive, strategic document that serves as a nonprofit's roadmap for its investments, ensuring a process that aligns investment decisions with the nonprofit's core mission and long-term objectives. Often just five to seven pages in length, an IPS should provide clear guidelines for managing an organization's most important financial assets.

Think of an IPS as a constitution for your organization's investment governance. It brings structure, accountability, and clarity to what can often be a complex and emotionally charged aspect of nonprofit management: investment strategy.

The Critical Components of an Effective IPS

A well-crafted IPS addresses several key areas.

First, it articulates the organization's **fundamental background** — its mission, tax status, financial history, and objectives for its funds. This foundational information helps contextualize all subsequent investment decisions.

The document then delves into **investment parameters**. What is the purpose of the organization's funds? What is the organization's risk tolerance (see Chapter 2)? What is its investment time horizon? What asset classes are acceptable or prohibited? These questions are not abstract; they have real-world implications for how funds are managed.

Portfolio asset allocation represents another crucial section of a good IPS. The asset allocation decision is one of the most important decisions an investor makes about their investment strategy. Here, a group's specific investment categories can be outlined — stocks, bonds, and any alternative investments like real estate or commodities. The document can also guide their strategic utilization. The policy might specify specific allocation ranges or tactical strategies, ensuring flexibility while maintaining clear boundaries.

A good IPS will also explicitly define the **duties and responsibilities** of all parties involved in a group's investment management. This can include a director, an investment committee, a treasurer, an external adviser, and others. By clearly delineating these roles, an IPS reduces potential confusion and creates accountability.

On multiple occasions, I've witnessed how a thoughtfully developed IPS can transform an organization's financial strategy, create unity, and provide confidence. Whether it's managing an unexpected donation, navigating volatile markets, or ensuring compliance with fiduciary standards, an IPS is a valuable tool.

A Team Approach

Creating a robust IPS is not a task to be undertaken alone. Those with institutional knowledge of the organization should ideally be involved. Those familiar with the organization's financials, bylaws, and operational aspects can be a great help.

A skilled financial adviser, particularly one with experience in the nonprofit sector, can provide helpful guidance as well. They bring an outside perspective as well as expertise and experience in crafting nuanced policies, understanding regulatory requirements, and helping organizations balance financial growth with mission-driven priorities.

In addition, by developing a long-term relationship with the same adviser, an organization can be confident that institutional knowledge related to the nonprofit's circumstances is expanded. Ultimately, it's beneficial when a policy is developed by a team rather than by a single individual.

Practical Considerations and Implementation

An IPS is not meant to be a static document. It should include provisions for regular review and potential modification. Markets change, and organizational priorities evolve. For these reasons, your nonprofit's investment strategy should be regularly monitored to adapt if necessary while remaining aligned with your organization's core principles.

Moreover, an IPS should address critical operational questions: How often will the portfolio be rebalanced? What benchmarks will be used to evaluate performance? How are donations, if applicable, to be handled?

YOUR FINANCIAL ROADMAP

An IPS is more than a bureaucratic "to-do." It's a strategic tool that can help your nonprofit achieve and maintain long-term financial health. By providing clear guidelines, reducing reactive decision-making, and helping create organizational continuity, an IPS allows not only your board, *but future boards as well,* to focus on what truly matters: advancing your nonprofit's mission.

Remember: Your financial assets aren't mere numbers. Those resources are the fuel that powers your nonprofit's critical work. An IPS helps ensure this fuel is managed with the same care, strategy, and mission-driven focus you bring to every other aspect of your organization.

PRACTICAL ACTION STEPS FOR BOARDS TO CONSIDER

1. **Assess your current investment approach** and identify gaps, such as whether an IPS exists.
2. **If an IPS does not exist, begin drafting one.**
3. **Outline** the organization's fundamental background information, roles and responsibilities, investment guidelines, and procedural processes.
4. **Schedule regular reviews** and be prepared to update the document as your organization grows and situations change.

CHAPTER 6

Creating a Sound Spending Policy

"You can have a master's degree in making money, but you will still wind up broke if you have a PhD in spending it."

- Orrin Woodward, *Launching a Leadership Revolution*

Dr. Pete Rodriguez sits in the board meeting of the National Society for Renal Research (NSRR), his brain buzzing with questions.

It's late 2021, and the nonprofit has just received an unexpected windfall: a $3 *million* donation from an eternally grateful kidney patient whose life was extended thanks to a clinical trial overseen by NSRR.

And despite the countless disruptions caused by the COVID-19 pandemic, NSRR actually came out of it in great financial shape. The usually costly annual meeting was switched to virtual, but attendance remained solid, and so did sponsorships. As a result, NSRR is in a somewhat unusual position of being very cash-heavy.

Pete's fellow board members are also lost in thought, each one fantasizing about this question: *What should we do with all this money?*

The options are tantalizing:

- Immediately fund new research programs.
- Hire additional staff.
- Upgrade laboratory equipment.
- Beef up the emergency reserves.
- Some combination of the above.

All the options are perfectly valid, and each has its own adamant supporter on the board. Spending is always enticing, but where might the board draw the line?

What a marvelous problem to have! Most nonprofit board members would be thrilled to be sitting in a board meeting like that! It's great to have a big year financially, but equally important to not live like a big year is the norm. Without a clear spending policy, a rare opportunity like this can quickly become a source of organizational tension. And it can lead to significant financial missteps.

THE SIGNIFICANCE OF A SPENDING POLICY

As we know in our personal lives, spending can be a lot of fun. However, it can easily get out of hand or leave you in a tighter position financially. Every medical nonprofit may face a time when donated funds or accumulated reserves can be strategically deployed to further support the organization's mission. A spending policy can provide prudent guidelines for leaders as they oversee how their organization responsibly uses its funds while also striving to maintain financial stability. This critical document can help balance the need for financial *flexibility* with the imperative of maintaining sound financial *discipline.*

A comprehensive spending policy dictates how much can be spent toward various specified purposes. It offers a thoughtful, structured approach to financial decision-making by establishing allowable spending amounts or ranges to, ideally, account for the impact of market fluctuations.

KEY CONSIDERATIONS IN DEVELOPING A SPENDING POLICY

A wise spending policy does multiple things:

- It carefully assesses and addresses multiple factors regarding the use of organizational funds. These factors include understanding the original purpose of various funds and gifts. Were they designated for certain purposes?
- It addresses what the spending is meant to help support or accomplish, and for how long the spending is meant to continue.
- It calls for an evaluation of general economic conditions, such as considering potential inflation or deflation impacts.

The policy also factors in the risk and return profile, as well as the organization's other available resources.

An approach might involve authorizing spending up to a specific percentage — for example, 3-5% — of a rolling multi-year average market value of reserves. Or maybe the spending amount is tied to a single factor, like inflation. Some policies may even combine the two as a "hybrid" approach. Large university endowments have led to this method receiving significant attention. This methodology is meant to smooth the data points so there's greater predictability, even when markets and investment values fluctuate year to year, and the assets that support it.

Prudent spending policies might also include provisions for exceptional circumstances. For instance, when a large gift is received, the policy might permit additional spending, such as allocating up to a certain amount of the substantial gift for a specific project or purpose.

What About Donor-Restricted Funds?

Occasionally, medical nonprofits receive donations with stipulations that the funds be used for specific purposes, earmarked for certain situations. Your spending policy might clearly articulate how these restricted funds will be managed differently from unrestricted assets. Or maybe there's a spending policy just for these funds. Either way, the spending policy may detail different purposes, objectives, considerations, spending rates, or more based on the particular circumstances of a given situation.

The Role of Flexibility

Effective spending policies incorporate language that gives organizational leadership some discretion. Permissive terminology such as "may spend up to..." provides flexibility during unexpected economic shifts or organizational challenges.

This flexibility ensures that a board can adjust its spending strategies in response to changing circumstances without being rigidly bound by predetermined allocations.

Practical Spending Considerations

When developing a spending policy, boards should carefully consider the following questions:

- What is the nature of our potential expenses? Are they fixed or variable?
- How do current organizational cash flows support potential spending?
- What are the timing requirements for anticipated expenditures?
- How will our proposed spending align with the organization's broader strategic objectives?

Remember, a well-crafted spending policy is so much more than a financial document. It's a practical and strategic guide that aims to ensure your nonprofit makes a meaningful impact now and for years to come.

PRACTICAL ACTION STEPS FOR BOARDS TO CONSIDER

To create an effective spending policy, your board should consider:

1. **Conduct a comprehensive review** of current financial resources and organizational goals.
2. **Consider the nature** of the spending your organization may be looking to do.
3. **Draft a policy** that provides clear guidelines, *even as it maintains healthy flexibility in spending.*
4. **Regularly review and update your spending policy** to reflect changing organizational needs and economic conditions.

CHAPTER 7

The Role of a Reserve Policy

"The time to repair the roof is when the sun is shining."

—John F. Kennedy, 35th President of the United States

In March 2020, the Geriatric Healthcare Alliance found itself in an unprecedented situation as the COVID-19 pandemic emerged.

The nonprofit had just opened a new Alzheimer's research facility and care clinic. GHA's annual meeting was a significant source of revenue, but with the pandemic, no meetings were scheduled for the foreseeable future, threatening to put a big dent in the group's financials.

While many medical nonprofits struggled to maintain operations during the lockdown, the GHA was uniquely positioned. Over the past decade, GHA has been intentional about building reserves. With larger windfalls or surpluses in given years, the group saved the surplus funds for the rainy day. They put policies into place to guide how much GHA would aim to have in reserve, how often it would evaluate whether to take or add to the reserves, and other factors. This prudent reserve policy became its lifeline.

Because GHA had built up and maintained liquid reserves over the prior decade, it was able to retain key staff, continue funding critical programs, and even expand its telehealth services at a time when in-person care was limited.

UNDERSTANDING TYPES OF RESERVES: BEYOND THE BASICS

When discussing organizational reserves, many new board members limit their thinking to "our checking account balance." But reserves should ideally include more than the checking account, given their importance to an organization (see Chapter 1).

When evaluating your group's reserve funds, you likely will want to consider how much you need (or want to have) for operating cash, excess savings, short-term investments, and long-term investment portfolios. Each of these "buckets" can play a key and distinct role in ensuring financial stability and mission fulfillment.

Operating reserves typically reside in your checking and savings accounts. As is the case with your own personal checking and savings accounts, funds in this "bucket" are meant for covering ongoing, day-to-day expenses, including short-term expenses. Therefore, risk should be minimized as much as possible.

Short-term investments are usually held in conservative vehicles such as money market funds or short-duration bonds, with a small component of equities. In this way, they can generate returns while providing the benefit of accessibility without being subject to greater levels of market risk where their value might be down at a time when your organization needs them.

Long-term investment reserves are often spread across various asset classes. This strategy provides growth potential and inflation protection for funds that won't be needed in the immediate future. Across all the segments of reserves, this is the area where the most risk can be taken.

RESERVE POLICY COMPONENTS

Just like with an IPS, a written policy that provides guidelines for current and future boards can be important. But where do you start?

Purpose. A great place to start is with the purpose of the funds at hand. Why do you have these funds? How are they meant to support the organization?

Objectives. What does your organization want these funds to do in the event they're called upon? Maybe they should pay for a one-time strategic expense or cover an unexpected budget deficit. Knowing the answer, or answers, helps inform one of the most common questions we hear: "How much should our organization hold in reserve?"

The answer actually has parallels to personal financial planning. Just as individuals are advised to maintain emergency funds, so are nonprofits, as they need sufficient reserves to weather unexpected challenges. How much your nonprofit should have in reserve can vary from organization to organization because the objectives and nature of those objectives can vary from organization to organization.

While a 12-month expense coverage is often regarded as a good general benchmark, your organization's specific circumstances should drive this decision. In the case of the Geriatric Healthcare Alliance, board members were relieved they had set aside 18 months of operational expenses — not just 12 — given the operational and strategic aspects their reserves needed to support.

Determining what's best for your nonprofit requires careful consideration of your revenue sources and their reliability. Organizations that are heavily dependent on annual events or seasonal activities may want to keep larger reserves than those with steady monthly income streams. If, for example, a significant portion of your annual revenue comes from two major fundraising events, it is wise to keep a larger amount in reserve in case fundraising slows.

Expense patterns are also a factor in these deliberations. Organizations with long-term venue contracts, equipment leases, or grant commitments should establish reserves that are sufficient to honor these obligations even during downturns.

Additionally, it's smart to consider your staff size and structure. Organizations with larger permanent staffs will benefit from having more substantial reserves than nonprofits with smaller, more flexible, and project-based workforces.

Additional Topics. Other topics commonly included in reserve policies include how reserves are funded (both initially and on an ongoing basis), what happens if there is a shortfall in reserves for a certain period of time, the process for reviewing the policy, and how, when, and why the organization may use reserves.

THE STRATEGIC IMPACT OF RESERVE PLANNING

Reserve policy is about more than risk management. Reserve planning is a strategic tool that helps shape an organization's overall financial approach.

A well-crafted reserve policy can influence investment decisions. It helps guide fundraising targets. It informs program expansion plans. What's more, having a good, clear policy can enhance donor confidence by demonstrating wise financial stewardship and long-term sustainability.

The reserve policy can help establish an investment strategy that balances your organization's liquidity needs with the potential for asset growth. The policy can help ensure your reserves are appropriately balanced to work as hard as possible while helping support the organization's mission.

Remember, strong reserves don't just protect against downturns; they also empower your organization to seize opportunities and expand its impact when the moment is right.

As the Geriatric Healthcare Alliance discovered, thoughtful reserve planning doesn't just enable you to survive a crisis. It can turn a potential disaster into an opportunity to better serve your constituents.

In the next chapter, we'll explore the other policies that can be impactful to an organization.

PRACTICAL ACTION STEPS FOR BOARDS TO CONSIDER

Here are four ways you can strengthen your organization's reserve position:

1. **Assess your current reserves across all categories:** operating cash, short-term investments, and long-term investments.
2. With your financial adviser, **evaluate your organization's specific risk factors and financial patterns** to get a good sense of appropriate reserve targets.
3. Make sure your written reserve policy specifies minimum requirements and outlines **clear guidelines for both using and replenishing your reserves**.
4. **Review and update your reserve policy annually**, adjusting for changing organizational needs and economic conditions.

CHAPTER 8

Creating Policies for Other Matters

"Someone's sitting in the shade today because someone planted a tree a long time ago."

- Warren Buffett, Chairman of Berkshire Hathaway

About a month ago, the board members of the Midwest Women's Health Foundation received the shocking news that the organization's long-time executive director, Margaret Worthy, had suffered an aneurysm and was in a coma. Her prognosis was unclear.

Within 36 hours, the nonprofit's board convened to appoint an interim director from within the organization ... then immediately faced a series of operational challenges.

Staff members found they were unable to transfer $250,000 from the nonprofit's investment account to cover a big grant commitment. The reason? Margaret had been the only person authorized to access the organization's account. The organization had never established a formal policy for alternate signatories.

What should have been a painless transaction morphed into a two-week ordeal. Emergency board meetings. Endless back-and-forth with the financial institution. And there was the embarrassment of discovering this delay meant that a grant recipient had to reschedule a medical conference, affecting about a dozen presenters and hundreds of attendees from all over the world.

The situation became even more complicated a week or so later when the board's financial advisory firm informed them that they couldn't execute additional desired trades because the account was still restricted.

By the time the board established new access protocols, the nonprofit was suffering from a damaged relationship with a grantee and membership that could have been avoided with clear policies on financial authority and contingency planning.

This scenario illustrates why explicit policies aren't just a good idea — they are an organizational imperative.

Let's look at a few policies your board should consider establishing.

ACCOUNT MANAGEMENT AND ACCESS CONTROLS

Prudent management extends beyond investment strategy; it also needs to include account oversight. Your board should carefully consider:

- Limiting account access to essential personnel.
- Diversifying multiple authorized personnel.
- Establishing clear protocols for account modifications and monitoring.
- Developing robust cybersecurity safeguards.

Limiting access to essential personnel defines who has authority to access accounts. This restricted access should be documented so current and future leadership have clear guidelines to reduce confusion. Establishing and documenting limited access also helps prevent unauthorized use and ensures that only designated individuals manage sensitive financial assets.

Change happens. Those in leadership roles today likely will move into different positions or ultimately stop serving on a board or committee. Staff or board turnover can create delays or risks in accessing an organization's funds. We've seen situations in which an organization had a past-president as an authorized signer, but the past-president hadn't been on the board in any capacity for years. There should be a process for promptly adding and removing users to maintain operational continuity and reduce the risk of control lapses during transitions.

The institution where your organization's money is held (often referred to as the "custodian") may have its own requirements as well. Understanding the complex or manual requirements custodians may have to change account access, such as notarized forms or wet signatures, upfront avoids delays in gaining access or completing necessary, and possibly urgent, transactions.

Your board might also consider cybersecurity concerns.

CYBERSECURITY CONCERNS AND PROTOCOLS

Medical nonprofits face unique cybersecurity challenges, particularly with sensitive financial and, in some cases, stakeholder-related data.

Below are a few protective measures you might consider to help safeguard your nonprofit's financial assets at a time when cybersecurity attacks are commonplace:

1. **Multi-Factor Authentication (MFA).** Implement robust MFA for all financial account access, requiring at least two verification methods beyond passwords. This approach significantly reduces unauthorized access risks by creating multiple layers of identity verification, making it exponentially harder for cybercriminals to breach accounts.
2. **Regular Cybersecurity Training.** Conducting quarterly cybersecurity awareness training for all staff helps create a human firewall against potential threats. These sessions can transform your nonprofit's employees from potential security vulnerabilities into active defenders. Your staff will learn how to recognize sophisticated phishing attempts, create and manage passwords effectively, and learn about the latest tactics used by cybercriminals.
3. **Financial Account Monitoring.** Set up comprehensive monitoring systems that provide real-time visibility into financial account activities. By implementing procedures that provide automatic transaction verification and fraud detection services, nonprofits can quickly identify and respond to suspicious activities, preventing potential financial losses and maintaining the organization's fiscal integrity.

By insisting on thoughtful, comprehensive policies, your organization can transform financial uncertainty into easily accomplished tasks. With agreed-upon protocols for common contingencies, you can protect your organization's mission, navigate economic challenges, and create sustainable pathways for ongoing efficiency.

PRACTICAL ACTION STEPS FOR BOARDS TO CONSIDER

1. **Identify key personnel** who should have access to accounts.

2. Create and communicate clear, transparent **account access and management protocols**.
3. **Do a tech audit** to uncover potential cyber vulnerabilities.

PART THREE

Investment Consulting

+ Continuity Coordination

+ Ongoing Collaboration

Nonprofit Health!

CHAPTER 9

Communication: The Critical Link Between Information and Action

"Put it before them briefly so they will read it, clearly so they will appreciate it, picturesquely so they will remember it and, above all, accurately so they will be guided by its light."

- Joseph Pulitzer, Publisher and U.S. Representative for New York

Dr. Alvin Boswell, board chair of the Frontotemporal Dementia Research Foundation, grimaces. Something about the group's quarterly investment report is off. The numbers didn't match what he remembers from the group's last meeting, and several key metrics appear to be missing.

When he calls FDRF's financial advisory firm to get clarification, he is connected to yet *another* unfamiliar voice — the third adviser he's spoken with in as many quarters.

This new contact is nice enough, but during the call, he seems to be catching up on the foundation's unique requirements as a medical nonprofit and its specific investment restrictions.

More concerning, the adviser can't explain why certain promised reports have not been delivered to the organization's auditor, who is now pressing up against some critical deadlines.

This scenario, while fictional, illustrates a common challenge many medical nonprofits face: poor communication. Whether an adviser is involved or not, when breakdowns occur, they can cascade into serious operational issues that adversely affect a board's ability to fulfill its organization's mission.

WHEN COMMUNICATION IS LACKING

When communication is subpar, the consequences are irritating at best and costly at worst:

- *Misalignment of financial priorities and risk tolerance.* A board may make decisions based on an incomplete understanding of the organization's financial position, thereby compromising the nonprofit's mission.
- *Delayed responses to financial challenges.* Without timely updates, a board can miss opportunities to change course, turning a small issue into a serious problem.
- *Uninformed strategic planning.* A board cannot plan to expand services or meet staffing needs and fundraising goals without timely financial data.
- *Compliance and reporting failures.* Medical nonprofits face specific regulatory requirements. A communication failure or mix-up can lead to missed filing deadlines or incomplete reporting.
- *Erosion of board confidence.* When communication is lacking, boards feel left in the dark to fend for themselves and are stuck worrying over the fundamental question, "Are we doing the right things?"

THE FOUNDATIONS OF EFFECTIVE FINANCIAL COMMUNICATION

At its core, good financial communication is about making sure the right people have the information they need, when they need it, from those who best understand the organization's unique circumstances. Effective communication encompasses at least five key elements.

1. Accuracy: Providing Dependable Information

The last thing a board needs is incorrect data. You can't make good decisions with information that's outdated, incomplete, or just plain inaccurate. This is especially true with investments, where there can be a lot of nuance. For example, performance is often much more complicated than just "We had this much then and have this much more now."

When you account for time periods, money added, money taken out, and the size of said cash flows, reporting can involve complicated calculations. You can also report performance based on certain factors being included or excluded, such as internal rate of return (IRR) versus time weighted return (TWR), so understanding how your performance numbers are, and should be, calculated is critical.

2. Frequency: Establishing a Reliable Rhythm

The frequency of communication ideally aligns with your organization's needs and decision-making cycle. Regular, scheduled interactions — whether monthly, quarterly, or according to another appropriate timeline — help ensure that your board stays informed, compliant, and can act promptly when needed. These touchpoints may consist of formal investment reviews, performance reports, market updates, and/or strategic planning sessions. Earlier, we discussed the idea that fiduciary responsibilities encompass leaders being regularly engaged and informed (see Chapter 2). Establishing a communication process is a great way to stay accountable and meet that requirement.

3. Consistency: Forging Strong Relationships

Just as important as accuracy and frequency is consistency in whom you're communicating with. Trust is key in any relationship, but when dealing with financials, it is paramount. A revolving door of those you communicate with isn't merely frustrating; it's flirting with trouble. Such a dynamic can impede your ability to act wisely and in a timely manner, especially when dealing with an organization, as new perspectives and preferences can easily be projected onto the situation. These new perspectives can be detrimental to your organization's overall financial health and effectiveness.

For example, where there's an adviser involved, but you're talking to person A one quarter, person B the next, then person C, each interaction requires precious time to get the new adviser up to speed on your nonprofit's unique situation, history, mission, and goals.

Such a situation is far from ideal. Ideally, there is a consistent relationship with parties who know your organization well. This will result in:

- More efficient meetings and communications, since your adviser understands your context.
- Better strategic guidance based on deep knowledge of your organization's mission and constraints.

- Faster response times during critical situations, as there's no learning curve to overcome, and a clear understanding of responsibility.

4. Content: Making Information Actionable

The content of communications needs to be comprehensive. Medical nonprofits often need multiple types of information throughout the course of a year, such as:

- Investment performance.
- Cash flow projections and liquidity assessments.
- Risk management updates and strategy recommendations.
- Regulatory compliance information.
- Market analysis and economic updates relevant to your sector.
- Documentation for audit and tax purposes.

However, it's not enough that an adviser provides the necessary information. It also needs to be presented in a format that can be quickly absorbed and understood. After all, it's difficult to take action if you don't understand the information, and never mind the fact that leadership is already juggling "who-knows-how-many" different demands, both personally and professionally.

5. Coordination: Ensuring Smooth Information Flow

A fifth critical aspect of communication is the ability to coordinate with other professional services providers. Many people are likely involved in an ongoing process. Who should take the lead and coordinate with everyone? How can that be done most effectively? Nonprofits commonly need to provide appropriate information to:

- Tax advisers and accountants.
- Legal counsel whenever financial matters have legal implications.
- Auditors during annual reviews.
- Key staff members who need access to specific financial information.

This coordination helps ensure that all parties have the information they need to serve your organization effectively and meet regulatory requirements.

At a "communications minimum," you want advisers who:

- Provide regular, jargon-free updates and insight tailored to your board's financial literacy level.
- Offer proactive alerts about potential issues before they become critical.
- Present clear explanations of how decisions will affect your organization's mission.
- Are available to answer questions between formal meetings.
- Deliver timely responses to inquiries from board members or leadership.
- Create understandable reports that highlight key metrics relevant to your organization's status and program sustainability.
- Articulate the implications of regulatory updates.
- Demonstrate an understanding of the unique challenges facing medical nonprofits, including reimbursement cycles and healthcare funding complexities.

Armed with the right information at the right time, and with the help of the right people, you'll better position your organization for long-term success. This is key to having a deep, lasting impact on the medical community you serve.

PRACTICAL ACTION STEPS FOR BOARDS TO CONSIDER

To ensure your organization is receiving the communication it needs to be effective, do the following:

1. **Review your current communication schedule.** Is it meeting your needs? Are there gaps that need to be addressed?
2. **Assess the quality and relevance of the information you're receiving.** Are you getting what you need to make informed decisions? Is anything missing?
3. **Create clear, detailed protocols for information sharing** between your key personnel and other professional service providers.
4. **Document your communication expectations** and review them regularly.

CHAPTER 10

Other Services: Building a Resource Network for Nonprofit Success

"Plans go wrong for lack of advice;
many advisers bring success."
-Proverbs 15:22

In 2023, the Richard Kirby Foundation (RKF) got off to a flying start.

It was established with a staggering $10 million gift and fueled by a noble mission: support groundbreaking medical research into neurodegenerative diseases. Led by a board of distinguished physicians and accomplished researchers, RKF's future seemed bright.

But two years in, the fledgling organization is facing challenges. The director and another key employee abruptly resigned last week. The reason? After two years of operation, the director and key employee were spending an exorbitant amount of time trying to find donors and handling issues around employee benefits. These tasks weren't exactly what they envisioned doing when they signed on, and they had just had enough.

A rigorous search for a new director is underway. At the same time, the board is trying to establish a retirement plan and find better medical coverage for RKF's employees. Meanwhile, the organization is short-handed.

And aside from the initial major donation, potential donors keep saying they just don't have the cash to give at this time.

The board of the Kirby Foundation is discovering — like so many nonprofit boards before it —that guiding an organization involves a lot of work. While labeled a "nonprofit," you're actually running a business, trying to make sure it is maximizing revenue and the benefits it provides to its own team.

THE VALUE OF A COMPREHENSIVE RESOURCE NETWORK

This is another area where a competent, proactive financial adviser can be beneficial. In addition to helping you manage your organization's investments, they can also function almost like a concierge. That is, they can connect your board to additional services and needed expertise across multiple domains.

In short, whether providing hands-on assistance or making strategic introductions to other professionals with more expertise, a competent adviser makes sure your organization has access to all the resources it needs for success.

Here are a few areas your organization may want to further explore, and who might be able to help.

Banking and Financing Resources

Your organization's banking relationship should involve more than basic checking and savings services. A savvy adviser will help you evaluate additional benefits offered by your financial institution and identify ways to optimize that partnership. This might include, for example, using a high-yield savings account to maximize returns on your nonprofit's operational funds or perhaps taking advantage of available lines of credit.

Charitable Giving

Cash and checks are the most common ways donors give to nonprofits. But donors have many other options for giving. For example[6]:

- *Stock Donations*: Donors give appreciated securities directly to nonprofits, receiving tax benefits while avoiding capital gains tax.
- *Donor Advised Funds (DAF)*: These function like a charitable investment account where donors receive immediate tax deductions for contributing to the DAF and can subsequently direct funds to chosen charities over time.

- *Qualified Charitable Distributions (QCD)*: This vehicle allows older individuals to transfer funds from IRAs directly to charities, satisfying required distributions while excluding that money from taxable income.
- *Charitable Trusts*: These structured giving arrangements can provide income to donors or charities for a set period, with remaining assets eventually transferring to the other party.

It's important to let donors know they have options; however, when these options involve complicated investment options, boards will benefit from the help of an expert.

Employee Retirement and Health Planning Expertise

As the Kirby Foundation discovered, a good employee retirement plan and excellent healthcare coverage represent more than just standard benefits — they're strategic tools for attracting and retaining talent.

Regular professional reviews of benefits help ensure employees receive optimal service, excellent investment options, adequate educational support, and ample health insurance plans.

Some firms can provide such employment benefit services; all of them can ideally connect you with specialized experts who can help you:

- Conduct comprehensive plan reviews to assess competitiveness and efficiency.
- Compare healthcare insurance plans and offer attractive coverage to your employees.
- Provide educational webinars and individual consultations for employees.
- Ensure compliance with ERISA (Employee Retirement Income Security Act) and other regulations.
- Evaluate how your current benefit package aligns with your organizational goals and industry standards.

REMEMBERING YOUR FIDUCIARY RESPONSIBILITIES

As we mentioned at the outset of this book, nonprofit board members are expected to live out the fundamental fiduciary duties of care, loyalty, and obedience. Managing organizational resources demands heightened scrutiny and clear, formal processes. For these reasons, you want a financial adviser who sees to it that your board adheres to its fiduciary duties. This may include:

- Targeted educational sessions.
- Regular reviews of investment policies and procedures.
- Guidance on documentation and decision-making processes.

To summarize: We've talked a lot about investments, but several other areas can be important. Your organization's success can depend on a number of factors similar to those in running a business. Organizations are often led by highly educated, intelligent leaders, but aspects of running a business are not always part of their expertise. And a well-connected financial adviser can be a resource beyond just investments for your board.

PRACTICAL ACTION STEPS FOR BOARDS TO CONSIDER

1. **Conduct a resource audit**. Review your organization's current professional relationships and identify any gaps in expertise or service.
2. **Evaluate your financial adviser's scope**. Can your current adviser assist with more of the services your organization needs?
3. **Develop a professional network map**. Document key contact points for various services (banking, legal, accounting, etc.) and ensure key personnel maintain these relationships.
4. **Schedule regular service reviews**. Set up annual reviews of key services, such as banking relationships and retirement plans.
5. **Invest in board education**. Establish a regular schedule for board training on fiduciary duties and best practices.

Conclusion

"You do not rise to the level of your goals.
You fall to the level of your systems."
–James Clear, *Atomic Habits*

Dr. Paulette Colvin never expected to find her life's calling in a boardroom.

A retired neuropsychiatrist, she joined the board of the Hilda Taylor Learning Disabilities Foundation somewhat reluctantly, viewing it as a nominal commitment. But after a few months, something shifted inside her. As she observed the nonprofit's work, she realized a profound truth: Being a board member is less about policy discussions and investment decisions and more about creating sustainable hope.

Paulette points to Marcus, a boy who struggled all through grade school because of a learning disability and who was homeless by age 13. She gets teary-eyed as she recalls how one of the nonprofit's grants helped Marcus overcome his many challenges.

Now 24, Marcus is completing his nursing degree because, as he puts it, "Those people believed in me and my potential. They wouldn't let me go."

His story is a testament to what happens when an organization strategically allocates its resources to create genuine, transformative change.

Then there's Robert Kendrick.

Paulette shakes her head in wonder as she thinks about the crusty old investment banker who spent decades chasing corporate profits. When he first donated to Hilda Taylor, it was a calculated decision. He was still a bit skeptical.

But as he began to see the impact of his contribution — how every dollar was carefully stewarded and strategically deployed — his whole attitude changed. He wasn't simply engaging in charity. He was investing in human potential. At a recent gala, Robert shared that for the first time in his life, "I feel like I'm creating true wealth. Not financial wealth, but social wealth that will continue to compound long after I'm gone."

These stories converge on a simple, powerful truth: Nonprofits are more than organizations. They are incubators of human potential. Behind every number on a spreadsheet, there exists the potential for a story that transcends the imagination.

This isn't hyperbole. The possibilities really are breathtaking. And the stakes couldn't be higher. This is why nonprofit success demands unwavering commitment, strategic planning, and careful stewardship.

And all of that requires a well-resourced, smooth-functioning board.

THE MEDIQUS FORMULA: A ROADMAP TO NONPROFIT HEALTH

Our formula for nonprofit success isn't about grand, sweeping gestures. It's about simple, smart "systems" (as James Clear calls them).

What's needed is consistency and intentionality across the three critical domains we've looked at in this book: investment consulting, continuity coordination, and ongoing collaboration.

When boards focus on these vital areas, their organizations are better positioned to handle changes in the investment world and their own world.

Investment Consulting Is More Than Just Numbers

A wise and healthy board moves beyond viewing investments as mere financial transactions. They see each investment decision as a strategic choice that reflects the organization's values, mission, and long-term vision. By understanding risk, diversifying thoughtfully, and maintaining robust reserves, a nonprofit board can create a strong financial foundation that will support its organization's most ambitious goals and avoid making mistakes due to panic or euphoria.

Continuity Coordination Provides Organizational Backbone

Smooth leadership transitions aren't accidental — they're the result of meticulous planning. Developing comprehensive policy statements, creating clear guidelines, and establishing transparent protocols ensures that an organization's mission continues seamlessly, uninterrupted, no matter what leadership changes occur.

Ongoing Collaboration Is the Connective Tissue of Success

It's impossible to do any big job without good information and good help. Healthy nonprofits have boards that enjoy access to both. They should have trusted, competent advisers who provide them with the data and connections they need to succeed.

PRACTICAL ACTION STEPS FOR BOARDS TO CONSIDER

As you close this book, consider these four immediate, actionable steps:

1. **Develop a Strategic Partnership.** If you don't have one already, seek out a financial adviser who demonstrates a genuine commitment to nonprofits and understands the unique challenges of mission-driven organizations.
2. **Conduct a Comprehensive Financial Review.** Schedule a deep-dive assessment of your current investment strategies, policies, and resource networks. Identify gaps and opportunities for improvement.
3. **Invest in Board Education.** Commit to ongoing financial literacy training. The more your board understands, the more effectively you can guard and grow your organization's resources. Again, your adviser can help.
4. **Create a Living Document.** Transform your thoughts and ideas about investing into a written, agreed-upon investment policy statement. Then turn this from a static document into a dynamic tool that evolves with your organization's changing landscape.

FINAL REFLECTION

Success in the nonprofit world isn't about perfection; it's about persistent, purposeful progress. By embracing the simple MEDIQUS formula, your board members can transform from passive observers to focused guardians of your organization's mission and potential.

Investment Consulting
\+ Continuity Coordination
\+ Ongoing Collaboration

Nonprofit Health!

Your attention to the financial matters discussed in these pages can be the difference between an organization that is constantly reacting and one that creates lasting, meaningful change.

In closing, let me reiterate: Your work as a board member is significant. Your decisions have the potential to make a profound difference in countless lives.

Who knows how far your impact will spread?

REFERENCES

1. The CFA charter and CFP designation are awarded by the CFA Institute and CFP Board, respectively, and do not imply endorsement. To learn the requirements for obtaining these, please see https://www.cfainstitute.org/programs/cfa-program and https://www.cfp.net/certification-process.
2. The individuals and organizations in this book are fictitious. The situations and events described are based on the real experiences of actual people and nonprofits.
3. Herman ML. Liability and the Board: What Governing Teams Need to Know. Nonprofit Risk Management Center. https://nonprofitrisk.org/resources/liability-and-the-board-what-governing-teams-need-to-know/.
4. Buffett W. How inflation swindles the equity investor. *Fortune Magazine,* May 1977. https://fortune.com/article/buffett-how-inflation-swindles-the-equity-investor-fortune-classics-1977/.
5. Brinson GP, Singer BD, Beebower GL. Determinants of portfolio performance II: an update. *Financial Analysts Journal.* 1991;47(3): 40–48. https://www.scribd.com/document/48454383/Determinants-of-portfolio-performance.
6. Applicability and appropriateness of a given method can vary. Please consult with your tax, legal, and/or financial adviser to determine which is best for you.

APPENDIX

Glossary of Financial Terms

A

Asset Allocation: The strategy of dividing investments among different asset categories, such as stocks, bonds, and cash, to balance risk and reward.

B

Benchmark: A standard or point of reference against which financial performance can be measured.

C

Charitable Endowment: A permanent fund established to provide ongoing financial support for a nonprofit organization.

Charitable Remainder Trust (CRT): A trust that allows you or other beneficiaries to receive income for life or a designated length of time, then donates the remaining assets to charity. The creator gets a partial tax deduction when the CRT is set up. Chosen investments within the trust grow tax-free, and the creator is able to support favorite causes after the income period ends.

Conflict of Interest: A situation in which a board member's personal or professional interests could potentially compromise their ability to make unbiased decisions for the organization.

Corpus: The principal amount of an endowment or investment fund, which should remain intact while generating income.

D

Diversification: Spreading investments across various financial instruments to reduce overall risk.

Donor Advised Fund (DAF): Think of a DAF as a charitable savings account. You make contributions of cash, stocks, or other assets to the fund and get an immediate tax deduction. You can then recommend grants from the fund to qualified charities over time, while investing the remaining assets, which are able to grow tax-free.

Due Diligence: The careful investigation of a potential investment or financial decision to confirm all material facts.

F

Fiduciary Duty: A legal obligation to act in the best financial interest of the organization, with honesty, loyalty, and care.

Financial Statement: A formal record of an organization's financial activities and position, typically including balance sheet, income statement, and cash flow statement.

G

Governance: The system of rules, practices, and processes by which an organization is directed and controlled.

I

Investment Policy Statement (IPS): A document that outlines the organization's investment goals, risk tolerance, and specific guidelines for managing investments.

Illiquid Assets: Investments that cannot be quickly converted to cash without a substantial loss in value.

Internal Rate of Return: The annualized implied discount rate calculated from a series of cash flows. In other words, a measurement of return that considers cash flows.

L

Liquidity: The ease with which an asset can be converted into cash without significantly affecting its value.

M

Mission-Aligned Investing: Selecting investments that not only provide financial returns but also support the organization's core mission and values.

N

Net Asset Value: The total value of an organization's assets minus its liabilities.

P

Portfolio: A collection of financial investments held by an organization.

Prudent Investor Rule: A legal standard requiring fiduciaries to make investment decisions as a sensible person would, considering the organization's purposes and circumstances.

R

Risk Tolerance: The degree of variability in investment returns that an organization is willing to withstand.

Return on Investment (ROI): A performance measure used to evaluate the efficiency or profitability of an investment.

S

Socially Conscious Investing (SCI): An investment strategy that considers both financial return and social/environmental good. Sometimes referred to as Socially Responsible Investing or Ethical Investing.

T

Total Return: The actual rate of return of an investment, including both capital gains and income generated.

Time Weighted Return: An investment's compounded rate of growth over a specific time period. While TWR measures the return on an investment, it does not account for the effect of investor cash inflows and outflows.

V

Volatility: The rate at which the price of an asset increases or decreases for a given set of returns.

Volatility Range: A volatility range is the expected range of ups and downs in an investment's value over time. For example, if an investment has a volatility range of 15%, that means its value typically swings up or down by up to 15% from its average price. Financial advisors use this to help clients understand how much risk they're taking on and to set realistic expectations about potential gains and losses.

W

Whistle-Blower Protection: Legal safeguards for individuals who report unethical or illegal financial practices within an organization.

www.ingramcontent.com/pod-product-compliance
Lightning Source LLC
Chambersburg PA
CBHW071357230926
51846CB00002B/578
9781960762498